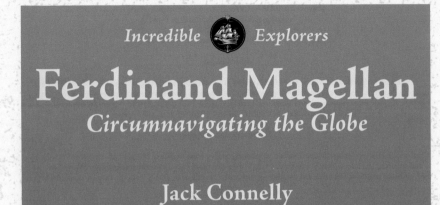

Incredible 🚢 *Explorers*

Ferdinand Magellan
Circumnavigating the Globe

Jack Connelly

Cavendish
Square

New York

Introduction

Expanding the World

The lifetime of Portuguese navigator and explorer Ferdinand Magellan coincided with Europe's age of exploration and discovery. For more than a century and a half, from 1415 to 1578, European nations sent hundred of explorations

The efforts of Portuguese explorer Ferdinand Magellan to sail completely around the globe forever changed the course of history and our understanding of the world.

out to expand their knowledge of the world. These explorations were driven somewhat by scientific curiosity, but the quest for riches was even more important. Explorers were seeking wealth for both themselves and the glory of their countries. Most of these trips did not produce groundbreaking information, and have been lost in history. The most successful trips have been recorded for posterity, and Magellan's trip around the world was one that would have significant ramifications for years to come. Just as earlier explorations had no doubt inspired Magellan to undertake his journey, news of his **circumnavigation** of the globe would fuel the dreams of future explorers.

The chance to take part in a grand adventure, to be cheered as a hero, and to find great riches—these were the reasons men left the safety of their homes to explore the unknown. Some, like Magellan, also wanted to learn the truth about world geography.

Where were other landmasses located? How big were they? Did the oceans all connect? Did different places have different climates? What about the people and animals who lived in these strange places? There were hundreds of questions to answer, and each answer led to new questions.

Most of the world was unknown to Europeans in 1480, the year Magellan was most likely born. No one knew for certain that Earth was round, although some people in ancient Greece had thought so almost 2,000 years before. No one had seen the whole world, so people could only guess at its shape. There were all kinds of stories about the mysteries of the world, too. Some people believed that monsters swam in the deep parts of the oceans and that a race of cannibal giants lived on strange islands.

About five hundred years before Magellan's fateful journey, northern Europeans had sailed to North America. The Vikings left their home in Norway about 1000 CE and explored the northeastern coast of North America, although they did not explore the interior of the land. This information never made it down to the southern half of the European continent, so both the Spanish and the Portuguese believed they were the first Europeans to reach these new lands.

Chapter 1
Exploring the Wider World

he man that would lead the first expedition to circumnavigate the globe, Ferdinand Magellan, was born about 1480 in Sabrosa, a city in the north of Portugal. His parents were **nobility**, which probably explains why

This map of Magellan's journey illustrates the boldness of voyage: He would have to sail across the Atlantic, around the southern tip of South America, into the unchartered waters of the Pacific, and back around the tip of Africa.

Magellan, at the age of fourteen, served in Lisbon as a **page** to the Portuguese Queen Leonor. During this time in his life, Magellan, as well as much of Europe, was hearing amazing stories of the Portuguese sailors that had studied the African coast. There were also stories about Spain's voyages of exploration to the New World led by Christopher Columbus and Vasco da Gama. These tales inspired many, including Magellan, to dream of beginning their own adventures and sailing journeys.

Born Fernão de Magalhães, Magellan would gain a different name, but not his most famous one, when he moved to Spain. There he would be known as Hernando Magallenes. Magellan is the English version of his last name, the version that most know him by today.

The Portuguese language is very similar to Spanish, but there are enough differences between the two, especially in spelling, to require translation. For instance, San Diego (Spanish) becomes São Diogo in Portuguese. Spain and Portugal had similar customs, religion, and government, but like two high schools in the same town, they were rivals.

Portugal faces the Atlantic Ocean on the Iberian Peninsula in southern Europe. It is a country about half the size of the state of Missouri. At the time Magellan lived, its population was about one million. For most of its history, Portugal has been overshadowed by its much larger neighbor, Spain. When Magellan was alive, Spain and Portugal were bitter enemies.

Across the southern coast of Portugal lies the **Strait** of Gibraltar and the continent of Africa. The earliest Portuguese navigators turned toward Africa to explore the coastline of that continent. Eventually, Portugal had strongholds all along the coasts of Africa, forcing Spain to seek a westward route to the rich trading strongholds of Asia.

When Magellan was a boy, his family lived in the small port town of Aveiro, about 150 miles (241 kilometers) north of Lisbon. Lisbon is the capital city of Portugal and was home to the country's king and queen. Ferdinand's father, Rodrigo, was a sheriff. This was an honorary position, which meant he didn't actually have to do the work of a sheriff. The family probably had some money or land inherited from relatives. Like most of Europe, Portugal had a system of nobility that proceeded from the king to dukes and lords and other titles.

The children of common people did not go to school, but the Magellans were considered minor nobility. They had no title but were high enough on the social scale for their sons to be educated. Magellan's mother was Alda de Mesquita, and nothing is known about her except her name. There were two other children in the family, a girl, Isabel, and a boy, Diogo.

Magellan's grandmother on his father's side belonged to the de Sousas, a noble family favored by the royal house. This was very important to young Ferdinand because it meant he could be appointed to the royal court.

Launching the Age of Discovery

At that time, Portugal's royal family controlled everything that went on in the country and all trade with foreign countries. Ambitious young men found it was wise to try to win the favor of the king and queen because that was the only path to wealth and importance in Portugal.

Although little is known about Magellan's boyhood, we can make some educated guesses about it. He lived in a small town on an inlet of the ocean and because fishing was an important part of the Portuguese economy, so we can imagine that he frequently walked to the docks with friends to watch the fishing boats come in or the trade ships load and unload. Perhaps he talked with sailors and fishermen and heard stories about storms at sea or learned about the kinds of boats tied up at the docks. Perhaps he wondered about what lands lay beyond the horizon or if the vastness of the ocean was unending.

Portugal's Prince Henry the Navigator sponsored the voyages of many explorers.

PRINCE HENRY THE NAVIGATOR

Prince Henry was the son of Portugal's King João I and Queen Philippa. Interested in the world beyond Portugal from an early age and inspired by reading about Marco Polo's travels to Asia, he began sponsoring voyages of exploration in 1418. Today, he is regarded as the initiator of the great Age of Discovery.

Becoming a Page

When he was about fourteen, Ferdinand, his brother, and a friend named Francisco Serrao went to Lisbon to be pages in the court of King João II and Queen Leonor. João II had become king when Magellan was one year old. He was the great nephew of Prince Henry the Navigator, who had begun the Age of Discovery. King João II believed, as did his uncle, that Portugal could be a great sea power.

At the court, pages were trained by the queen's brother, Manuel. His job was to ensure that the pages were dressed and fed well. Pages served as assistants to the royal family. They did errands, learned court manners, and were present at royal functions. If they worked hard and made no enemies, they could become apprentices in certain professions. When they graduated, they frequently went into the military as high-ranking officers. They could also receive scholarships and become educated at the university, or they might even become advisers to the king. As long as they stayed on the king's good side, they might be given favors—land and money, or positions as ambassadors to a neighboring royal court.

It was not always easy to stay on the king's good side. There were many courtiers, or people who attended the court, and many different personalities. Some were trusting and kind; others were hostile or jealous. As Magellan found out, it was impossible to please everyone at court. Loyalties shifted from day to day. Someone who was a friend on Monday could be an enemy by Thursday. Some people who thought they'd been slighted never forgave or forgot the offense; others didn't let anything bother them. His good spirit allowed Magellan to advance to higher positions.

Manuel and King João II did not trust each other and frequently were at odds. Magellan was loyal to the king and obeyed him, even when that made Manuel angry. In 1495, João II died, and because the king had no son, Manuel became the king. As king, Manuel remembered that Magellan had preferred João II, and Manuel carried this grudge for the rest of his life.

Sailing into the Unknown

There were very few books in Europe at the time of Magellan and practically no libraries. Before the invention of the printing press in 1450, books had to be copied by hand, which took a long time. Even after books were printed, only a few volumes were printed at a time. Books were kept in universities or monasteries. These libraries were private, open only to the few who were wealthy and educated. Most ordinary people did not know how to read or write.

Very few people traveled even for short distances because it was expensive, uncomfortable, and dangerous. There was no notion of a "global economy," and very few people believed in seeking out anyone outside their own circle of family and friends. They were satisfied to stay at home.

There were no precise maps, as we know them today, with distances calculated. For hundreds of years, **cartographers** had made fanciful drawings of the world as they imagined it, with sea serpents in the ocean and lands where monsters lived, but they were only guesses, much like today's science fiction stories about life on other planets.

Around 1500, all the new information from the voyages of Christopher Columbus, Bartolomeu Dias, John Cabot, and other explorers was assembled to create a map of the world. The lands new to Europeans included North America, South America, the West Indies, Japan, and China. These maps were interesting to look at, but without any sense of distance, they were not very helpful to navigators.

In 1500, there was no common idea of geography. Germans saw the world in one way, Chinese in another, and Portuguese in yet another. The most important question for them all was whether the oceans were connected. If they were, it would be possible to sail around the world and come into contact with every country with a coastline. No continent, country, or island would be isolated.

While he was a student, Magellan learned reading, writing, religion, arithmetic, music, dancing, horsemanship, and fencing, which was the gentleman's way of solving arguments. He also studied algebra, geometry, astronomy, and navigation, all of which helped him to develop the skills he would need on his expeditions.

After Magellan finished his time as a page, he became a paid palace employee. He probably worked as a clerk for the India House, the agency that regulated trade. In the India House building, next door to the palace, maps, ship logs, and reports of voyages were stored. As a clerk, Magellan would have been able to study them. He also would have learned how to outfit an expedition. By reading the accounts of other voyages, he could decide which instruments, arms, supplies, and goods for trade would be needed.

He may have come across information about a strait between two oceans. The strait was something he had wanted to find for a long time; he thought it would be shorter, easier, and calmer than

Pedro Álvarez Cabral landed on the eastern coast of South America in 1500, claiming the land he found there for Portugal.

taking the route around the tip of South America. It was not known at the time if a route around South America was even possible. It might have been that South America went all the way to the South Pole, as many people thought at the time.

Thanks to the encouragement of King João II and then of King Manuel, Lisbon was a center for trade. Ships filled with people of many nationalities crowded the docks with flags from Holland, England, Belgium, France, Greece, and Germany. African slaves were also evident. In fact, Portugal is credited with starting the slave trade.

Everyone in Lisbon, including Magellan, would have heard of the successful voyage of Christopher Columbus in 1492, the journey of John Cabot to the New World in 1497, and Portugal's own Vasco da Gama and his voyages to India. Magellan probably stood among the crowd of people who waited on the docks in 1499 as two of da Gama's ships returned to Lisbon from India. One ship was loaded with spices, rare woods, and jewels, all purchased in Indian markets.

While Columbus had made the first visit to the New World in the name of Spain, it wasn't long before the Portuguese were also staking a claim to the continents of the New World. Pedro Álvares Cabral landed a fleet of thirteen ships on the eastern coast of South America. Cabral named the land Brazil after a type of wood his team found in the area. The year was 1500, and a twenty-year-old Magellan no doubt heard the amazing tales of the rich land, bizarre animals and plants, and new people that Cabral had encountered. Reviewing Cabral's maps of the ocean and the new land, Magellan was undoubtedly inspired to follow the explorer's footsteps and seek out new lands on his own.

European nations frequently battled over control of trade routes for rare and valuable commodities, such as spices.

Ferdinand Magellan

Chapter 2
The
Spice Wars

ack in Magellan's time, European nations battled for control of spice routes. At the time, nations considered almost anything made from plants they could not grow domestically "spices." The most popular were items such as nutmeg, pepper,

cinnamon, clove, and mace. Farmers had to slaughter their animals each fall because they could not harvest enough grain to feed the cattle through the winter. Without refrigeration, the meat would spoil, so farmers had to smoke and pickle the meat to make it last. These exotic and desired spices helped keep the meat flavorful. In addition, without indoor plumbing, the aromatic spices were used to keep the air perfumed.

Owning spices was a status symbol for the wealthy. One of the most sought-after spices at the time was nutmeg. Wealthy people would bring their own silver nutmeg graters with them when they went out to dinner. To show them off, some wore these graters like jewelry. Some men had the little sterling silver boxes engraved with their initials.

Many spices were used as medicine. Twenty-six different spices appeared in prescriptions for various diseases. Cloves were a remedy for chest coughs, headaches, and earaches. Today, oil of cloves is still frequently used for toothaches. Some spices were also thought to be a protection against contagious diseases. By sprinkling powdered cloves on their clothes, people thought they could keep away colds and the flu.

Wanting spices was just part of the desire for the good life. Wealthy people also wanted jewelry, silks, tapestries, fine porcelain or china, and anything else that seemed luxurious and made them feel important. These things were not available in Portugal or anywhere in Europe. They had to come from the East. Merchants recognized that there was a fortune to be made in trade.

Arabian traders had a monopoly on the spice trade in the fifteenth century. The main market for Eastern goods was Alexandria, Egypt. In order to keep their supplies a secret, Eastern traders wouldn't tell Europeans where they originally found their spices. Instead, they made up fantastic stories about their locations, saying

Ferdinand Magellan

they grew in dangerous places and were guarded by terrible beasts.

European traders, however, did not believe the stories. They heard rumors of islands, somewhere in the Indian Ocean, where spices, especially nutmeg, mace, and cloves, grew abundantly on trees and bushes. All one had to do was go there, pluck off the seeds, and fill up the holds of ships. Then they could sail back to Europe and become very wealthy.

The Spice Islands came to be called the Moluccas. Today, they are part of Indonesia. The Indian Ocean lies between the coast of eastern Africa and Malaysia, Indonesia, and Australia, which form a barrier to the east. All of the lands in the Indian Ocean, including the hundreds of islands as well as the subcontinent of India and southwest Asia,were then called the East Indies.

Prince Henry set the course for Portuguese spice hunters. He felt that all the spices of the Orient should come to Lisbon, bringing prosperity to Portugal. The Portuguese wanted to control the East Indies not only for the trade goods but also to convert the

The Moluccas, or Spice Islands, were the target of many European sailors hoping to become wealthy off of the spice trade.

Native people to Christianity. Their strategy was to defeat the alliance of Arabs, Italians, and Indians who already controlled the spice trade in India. Their first step was to use force to set up military bases at points around India and the east coast of Africa.

In 1505, at the age of twenty-five, Magellan joined the "spice wars." King Manuel named Dom Francisco de Almeida the first Portuguese viceroy, or governor, of the Indies. Magellan sailed as a general hand with Almeida's fleet, which contained twenty-two ships and 1,500 men. Their goal was to explore and conquer India.

In their attempt at conquest, the Portuguese fought several battles with the Arabs and Indians. Magellan was wounded twice in battle, in 1506 and in 1509. He earned a reputation as a brave fighter. He was promoted to captain in 1510 and took part in expeditions that captured the kingdom of Malacca in the Malay Peninsula in 1511.

Battling the Arabs and the Moors

With their success of capturing Malacca in 1511, the Portuguese won control of the gateway to the Far East. This event shattered the centuries-old Arabian monopoly. By then, the Portuguese were in control of the spice trade of the Malabar Coast of India, Ceylon, Java, and Sumatra, where they fought with the Arabs for control of the pepper trade. From India and Ceylon, they brought cardamom, cinnamon, and ginger to Europe.

Magellan spent about a year in Malacca, gathering information from merchants and from the crews of Chinese ships, anchored in the harbor. It was there he learned that his boyhood friend, Francisco Serrao, had located the Spice Islands and was living there in the Moluccas. He had even married a daughter of the sultan, or king. Serrao sent Magellan a letter telling him how wonderful the islands were and how great the opportunities were for trading.

In Malacca, Magellan acquired a slave named Enrique, who would remain with him for the rest of his life. Apparently Enrique knew many languages because he served as translator for Magellan. He may have been born in the Philippine Islands, as he gave Magellan much valuable information about that area.

Before Magellan could join his friend in the Moluccas, King Manuel sent him to Morocco in North Africa, along with 15,000 Portuguese soldiers, to put down a rebellion by the Islamic Moors. Magellan was badly wounded in a battle in the small town of Azamor, where a lance had pierced his knee. He limped because of this injury for the rest of his life. European soldiers wore armor then, but did not usually wear leg armor in battle because it was so heavy and bulky that it slowed them down.

For his bravery in this fight, Magellan was promoted to quartermaster-major. This was a prestigious post, and some of the older officers were jealous. That may have been the reason why officials charged Magellan with illegally trading with the Moors a few years later. This was a very serious charge because it amounted to treason, as the Moors were enemies of the Portuguese. Magellan claimed he was innocent. After an investigation, the army agreed, dropping the charges against him.

The idea that Magellan, with his strong Catholic background, would trade with Muslims was almost impossible to comprehend. The hostility between Christians and Muslims was intense at the time. Each group believed that theirs was the one true religion. Each accused the other of being infidels, or nonbelievers, and even devils. Furthermore, the Moors had invaded Portugal in the eighth century and had remained there for 400 years. The Portuguese battled long and hard to get them out. Even by 1500, they had not forgotten their struggle.

Portugal and the Moors

The people native to Portugal had a long and bitter rivalry with the Moors. This conflict dated back centuries. Just as the Catholics of Spain and Portugal believed it was their duty to convert the Native people of the New World to Christianity, the Moors believed that their god, Allah, wanted them to spread the Muslim faith throughout the world. In 711 CE, a Moorish army led by Tāriq ibn Ziyād invaded and conquered the Iberian Peninsula, beginning centuries of occupation of both Spain and Portugal. The Moors also occupied parts of France and Italy.

Despite having a reputation as barbarians among Christian Europeans, the Moorish occupiers did much to advance science, medicine, mathematics, geography, and architecture during their time in Portugal. Some Islamic inventions, such as the **astrolabe**, would prove to be valuable during Portugal's later years as a naval superpower. These advances were not limited to Muslims, as both Christians and Jews were permitted to exercise their respective faiths during the Muslim occupation of the Iberian Peninsula.

Eventually the Christians of both Portugal and Spain managed to reclaim control of their respective nations from the Moors. Although much of their influence, particularly in architecture, was destroyed after they were forced out, some Moorish-inspired design remains present in Portugal today.

Ferdinand Magellan

Although the idea that Magellan was a traitor was unlikely, King Manuel still held a grudge against him. He acted as if he believed the charges and fired Magellan from government service. Terribly disappointed, bewildered, and resentful, Magellan realized the king would never allow him to head an expedition to the Spice Islands. His career as a Portuguese explorer was over.

It was unlikely that Magellan would ever again command an expedition for his homeland. He did not, however, find himself able to give up his dreams of sailing to unknown lands so easily. In order to keep exploring, Magellan was going to have to make a drastic change and renounce his citizenship in order to explore under the flag of a new nation. He decided to travel to Spain and establish a new home. He was on his own, away from his friends and family, but time would show the wisdom of this difficult move.

The Moors left a permanent mark on the Portuguese countryside, constructing impressive fortifications during their occupation, such as this one in the southeast.

Chapter 3

Putting Together the Expedition

Magellan's move to Spain came at a time when his home country and his newly adopted home were in the middle of a great naval rivalry. Both nations were trying to claim and colonize as much

To avoid a war between Portugal and Spain, Pope Alexander VI issued the Treaty of Tordesillas, which divided the New World between the two countires.

Ferdinand Magellan

territory as possible for wealth and glory. Fearing war between two fervently Catholic nations, Pope Alexander VI tried to pacify the two countries with the 1494 Treaty of Tordesillas. This agreement set a **line of demarcation** down the Atlantic Ocean. Everything east of this line would belong to Portugal and everything west of the land would be the property of Spain. Other European nations, such as England, France, and the Netherlands, were not involved in the dispute at that point. That would, however, change over the next few centuries.

Although Europeans knew where the Spice Islands, called the Moluccas, were by 1517, no officially sponsored expedition had landed there to claim them. The Treaty of Tordesillas stated that if the islands were discovered by going east, they belonged to Portugal. If they were discovered and held from the west, they belonged to Spain.

From the time of Christopher Columbus the Moluccas were discovered and held from the west, so they belonged to Spain. King Ferdinand and Queen Isabella had organized the Casa de Contratacíon, or the House of Trade, to license all ships, whether for trade or exploration. The Casa was made up of Spanish merchants who were very interested in getting to the Spice Islands before the Portuguese. Those in the Casa decided where ships would go and who would be aboard them.

Magellan knew he had to make friends with the men in the Casa. He stayed with Diego Barbosa, an important official in Seville who may have been an old friend. Barbosa was one of Magellan's strongest supporters and introduced him to many Casa members.

Soon after moving to Spain, Magellan married Beatriz Barbosa, Diego's daughter, an action that proved he intended to stay. Although they were not married long before he left for his voyage, he generously provided for her and their infant son, Rodrigo, in his will. In his will, he also left ten percent of all his assets, called a tithe, to the Catholic Church.

In February 1518, Magellan felt he was ready to approach the king with his proposal to find the Spice Islands. He and Rui Faleiro, a Portuguese cosmographer, or star mapper, journeyed to the Spanish court at Valladolid in the region of Castile to seek the help of King Charles I.

Charles was only sixteen years old when his grandfather, King Ferdinand, died. As heir to the throne, Charles was brought to Spain from Belgium, where he had been attending school. When Magellan approached him, he was eighteen and had been in Spain less than six months. His intelligence made up for his lack of experience, and he was very interested in learning more about exploration. In 1519, he would become Charles V, Holy Roman Emperor over most of Europe.

On the way to Valladolid, the impulsive Faleiro argued with the level-headed Magellan about how they would petition the king. Faleiro seemed to be more interested in enriching

Stripped of his title and power in Portugal, Magellan decided to petition King Charles I of Spain (above) to sponser his voyage.

Ferdinand Magellan

himself than in bringing glory to Spain. The men were joined by a man named Armanda, a merchant from the Casa. Armanda thought Faleiro, who suffered periods of madness, acted foolishly, and he distrusted him.

Most of the Spanish merchants supported Magellan's plan. Not only would it enrich Spain, but it would also keep Portugal from getting richer. Although these merchants had supported Columbus during his first two voyages, he had disappointed them. Columbus had brought them no new rich markets. They thought Magellan's voyage would be more successful. In addition, many merchants favored Magellan's down-to-earth personality.

In Portugal, meanwhile, King Manuel had changed his mind about Magellan. He was finally willing to listen to Magellan's proposal, but it was too late. Magellan refused to return, even though he'd heard that the Portuguese agents would try to stop him from sailing under a Spanish flag.

Magellan's presentation on February 23, 1518 impressed everyone at the court of King Charles I. The would-be explorer brought maps, **charts**, letters of support from geographers, and specific plans. He demonstrated Faleiro's new methods of **celestial navigation**. He didn't make wild promises, as other explorers had done. He stood tall like a trained soldier and looked everyone in the eye.

Magellan said he wanted to find Balboa's Sea, which is now the Pacific Ocean, which he thought would take him to the Spice Islands. Nuñez de Balboa had glimpsed the ocean from a mountaintop in what is now Panama. He could tell it was a different body of water than the one he had sailed across, which was the Atlantic, to get to South America. A report from another exploration off the coast of Brazil had convinced Magellan that any southwest passage to Balboa's Sea would be west of the line of demarcation. If such a passage existed, it would belong to Spain, not Portugal.

Magellan presented his ideas with authority. Columbus had spent seven years trying to win the support of the Spanish crown. It took Magellan only one month. On March 22, 1518, King Charles agreed to Magellan's proposal.

Magellan and Faleiro were appointed joint captains general of an expedition directed to seek a Spanish route to the Moluccas. They were given the authority to govern any lands they discovered and were to receive a one-twentieth share of the net profits from their venture. Eventually, Faleiro was judged too high-strung to be allowed on a ship and was dropped from the roster.

Magellan's Fleet

The Spanish merchant Armanda bought five well-worn **carracks** (merchant ships) for the expedition. They were named

Bankrolled by the Spanish King, Magellan departed Seville, Spain, in 1519, leading five well-stocked ships intent on exploring the wider world.

Victoria, *Concepción*, *San Antonio*, *Santiago*, and *Trinidad*, which was the flagship. The ships were small but wide in the beam, built to hold trading goods.

Each ship had three masts. These were the main, foremast, and mizzenmast. A bowsprit was carried in case an additional sail was needed. Most of the sails used were square, but there were also a few lateen, or triangular, ones. The ships carried longboats and launches, which were stowed on the main deck and took up a lot of room. These rowboats were used as taxis to go from one ship to another or to go from the ship to the shore.

The decks and holds were stocked with gear, supplies, gifts for the people they would meet, and **armaments**. Among their arms were cannons, 5,600 pounds of gunpowder, arquebuses, or old-fashioned rifles, swords, javelins, lances, crossbows, and more than 4,200 crossbow bolts.

Their food was very plain. It consisted of salted meat, rice, biscuits, beans, almonds, and raisins. They brought salted fish and cheese for special occasions. Barrels of water and wine were stored above and below decks.

For the Native people they expected to meet, the crewmen brought mirrors, knives, fishhooks, velvet, ivory, brass bracelets, and perhaps the most popular item, 20,000 small bells. They would be used for trading as well as gifts.

Magellan supervised the hiring of the crew. Some were his choice, such as the thirty Portuguese seamen, for instance, while others were appointed by the Casa. The five ships had a combined total of about 270 men of various ethnic groups, mostly Spanish. There were also men from England, Asia, Ireland, Greece, Portugal, France, and Italy. The smallest crew, made up of thirty-two men, was on the *Santiago*. The largest crew, sixty men, was on the *Trinidad*.

The Ships of Magellan's Era

All the ships during Magellan's time were made of wood. Wood floats, but it also rots. It can break up in a storm and is food for rats and shipworms. Barnacles cling to a wood surface and make it heavier, reducing the ship's speed. Boats had to be constantly maintained during a voyage. Crewmembers were always patching holes in the hull or swabbing the deck with seawater to prevent rot.

All ships were powered by the wind through the use of sails. Smaller boats were powered by manpower, also known as rowing. Steam, gasoline engines, electric batteries, and nuclear power all came much later.

The ships were built for carrying trade goods, not for the comfort of the crew. Around 1470, the major countries of Europe, which were England, France, Spain, Portugal, Venice (now part of Italy), and Holland—began to build larger merchant ships to search for a trade route to the East. They wanted to reach India, Ceylon, the East Indies, and Malaysia, and bring trade goods back to Europe. They could not trade by land, as that would involve costly wars. Instead, they needed to find efficient waterways. This was the reason the Age of Discovery began.

Most of the crew were **ordinary seamen**, but there were also barbers, who acted as doctors in addition to cutting hair, chaplains, coopers,who repaired barrels and did carpentry, caulkers, and gunners. These men signed on because they needed work.

The officers, on the other hand, had different motives for joining the expedition. Most wanted to become wealthy and powerful and to work their way up to become court favorites. Two officers are remembered today for their part in the voyage: Juan Sebastián de Elcano (or del Cano), who was originally the

28

master of the *Concepcion*, and Juan de Cartagena, who had the command of the *San Antonio*.

Cartagena hoped to become inspector general of the entire fleet, with Magellan under him. Instead, King Charles made Magellan knight commander, a post of honor, with the title captain general. Cartagena never got over his disappointment. He refused to acknowledge Magellan's authority and tried to get the other Spanish officers to disobey him as well.

Also on board was Antonio Pigafetta, an Italian, who may have been a spy for his government or simply a sightseer. Pigafetta kept an extensive diary that tells us much about the voyage and Magellan. Some of the experiences he wrote about, however, are too fantastic to be believed today. In his diary, he wrote that he wanted to go with the expedition because he was "desirous of seeing the wonderful things of the ocean."

The five ships were not ready for several months, so they remained in Seville as the crew made final preparations. Finally, in early August of 1519, the ships sailed from Seville to the ocean port of Sanlúcar via the Guadalquivir River. In the port city, additional final preparations had to be made before the fleet could traverse the Atlantic. Soon all was ready, and the historic journey began.

Chapter 4

Heading for South America

The initial part of Magellan's journey followed the same path as Columbus's had more than twenty-five years earlier. The fleet stopped at the Canary Islands, a colony under Spanish rule. The cluster of islands was often used as

Magellan's fleet stopped at the Canary Islands, a Spanish colony off the western coast of Africa, to stock up on supplies for their long journey around the world.

Ferdinand Magellan

staging grounds for Spanish expeditions to the New World. There, the convoy was able to stock up on food and water for the crew, and pitch and wood to make any needed repairs on the ship.

While they were still in the Canaries, a ship arrived from Sanlúcar with an urgent message for Magellan from his father-in-law, Diego Barbosa. Barbosa warned Magellan that some of his captains had bragged while they were still in Seville that they would remove Magellan from his command one way or another.

Magellan sent a reply back. He wrote that he would give his captains no cause to revolt against him. Instead, he would listen to their complaints and try to resolve whatever was bothering them. He wanted to cooperate with everyone on the voyage. Barbosa showed this reply to members of the Casa, and they liked Magellan's cool-headedness. Showing it to them was a wise decision. When problems later arose between Magellan and his officers, the court knew that Magellan did his best to be fair.

As soon as the five ships were well stocked, they left the Canary Islands. Remembering the warning from his father-in-law, Magellan decided not to tell the officers in the other ships of his exact route. He told them simply to follow him—to follow his flag by day and the lanterns on the ship by night. When the ocean was calm, the men on board the different ships often shouted information to each other. There was no other system of communication, not even the use of signal flags. Not being told where they were going angered the captains, but they followed Magellan's lead for the first several weeks.

Routines of the Fleet

Once they were under sail, the sailors kept to a strict shipboard routine. Discipline was a crucial part of life at sea. Every crewmember was given a job and was expected to do it well and without complaint. Idlers were punished.

As captain general, Magellan had authority over everyone, including the other captains. Each ship's captain had authority on his vessel over the duties assigned there. The master oversaw the housekeeping details on the ship, keeping it clean and in good repair, and the mate assigned chores to the seamen to keep the ship seaworthy.

The ships were steered by a tiller or lever that extended from the rudder through an opening in the stern, or the back of the boat. The man who controlled the tiller was called the helmsman. He worked below the deck and could not see out, so the pilot on the quarterdeck shouted commands to him through a hatch. In setting the course, the pilot used dead reckoning, which meant he watched where he was going and used known landmarks to determine the ship's location and course. He also received instructions from the captain based on star charts.

The crew was divided up into watches. They had to watch for anything and everything, since they had no radar. Did that cloud on the horizon look like an approaching storm? Was that disturbance in the water a whale that might collide with the ship? Were other ships nearby? Once they started moving into uncharted waters, they had to be especially attentive, for no one knew what to expect.

One four-hour watch was assigned to the port, or left, side of the ship and another to starboard, or the right side. The crew used sand clocks, or hourglasses, to time their watches. Each sand clock took thirty minutes to empty, so for a four-hour watch, it had to be turned eight times. It was against regulations for a sailor to hold the hourglass because the warmth of his body made the sand run faster and the time of his watch shorter.

The captain always took the first watch of the night. At the end of his watch, a mate sang a song:

On deck, on deck, gentlemen of the starboard watch,

Hurry up on deck, Mr. Pilot's watch

Right now; get up, get up, get up!

The daytime work for the sailors was never-ending, especially swabbing, or mopping, the deck to keep it free of salt water and pumping out the bilges. The bilges were the areas below the waterline where dirty water collected. Too much water could sink the ship. Sailors also had to take care of the sails and the rigging—the system of ropes that kept the sails in place. A torn sail or frayed rope had to be repaired at once. Sailors were constantly searching for leaks, damage done by rats and shipworms, and any other signs of trouble. Their lives depended on keeping the vessels in shipshape.

There were no cooks on board. When the weather was good enough, apprentice seamen cooked on deck over a sand bed in the firebox. When the weather was bad, meals were catch-as-catch-can for the seamen. Cabin boys, who were like domestic servants, prepared meals for the officers.

The only person with any privacy was the captain, who had a small cabin in the forecastle in front of the ship. The men slept on deck where and when they could. When the weather was bad, they sometimes went for days without sleeping at all.

Under Magellan's command, either a chaplain or the captain conducted formal religious services every day on each of the ships. This was not true for other expeditions.

South to the Equator

As they headed south toward the **equator**, the five ships remained close to the coast of Africa to avoid the Portuguese-held

Cape Verde Islands. Magellan feared an attack by his former countrymen to stop the voyage.

They passed the landmark mountain of Sierra Leone, located on the western coast of Africa. It then began to rain in furious squalls. It rained so hard and for so many days that the expedition's stores began to mold and rot. The crew had trouble sleeping as well. Magellan then put the crew on half-rations to conserve the food.

During one particularly bad storm, the men witnessed Saint Elmo's fire—a phenomenon of atmospheric electricity that sometimes gathers about the masthead of ships and on riggings. Although similar to lightning, Saint Elmo's fire forms cloud-like shapes rather than zigzags in the sky. In Magellan's day, these shapes were interpreted as religious signs, a cross or the face of a saint, for instance. The men took the appearance of Saint Elmo's

During the voyage, Magellan's men saw the atmospheric phenomenon known as St. Elmo's fire. The men took the burst of light as a good sign.

Ferdinand Magellan

fire as a good omen, and after the sighting the sea became calm. Unfortunately, it was too calm, and the ships became stuck in the doldrums, where the wind did not blow. For weeks they progressed only a few miles a day, the ship only riding the ocean waves.

By sailing in a diagonal line across the Atlantic, they reached the coast of Brazil in November. This area was familiar to Magellan thanks to stories he had heard of earlier explorations. He'd also studied the maps of the coast while he had been in Lisbon.

The crew sailed into Rio de Janeiro's natural harbor, where they saw parrots, monkeys, and other exotic animals and plants. The Tamojós, who were native to the area, had known the earlier Portuguese explorers and swarmed onto the decks of the ships offering chickens, fish, and garden produce in exchange for fish-hooks, knives, combs, or mirrors. One small bell was traded for a whole basket of sweet potatoes.

Magellan was concerned the entire time his crew stayed in Brazil. Although the weather was warm and sunny, Magellan feared attacks by his former Portuguese countrymen. He ordered the crew to speed through all repairs to the ships and to begin sailing south as soon as possible. The crew finished repairs by Christmas Eve, celebrated the holiday aboard the ships, and headed down the coast of South America. Magellan was ready to explore everywhere to find a river or channel to reach the ocean Balboa had seen.

Chapter 5
Sailing Around South America

nce the exploration passed eastern Brazil, Magellan and his crewmen had entered Spanish territory. Under the terms of the Treaty of Tordesillas, the Portuguese no longer had a claim on any new land

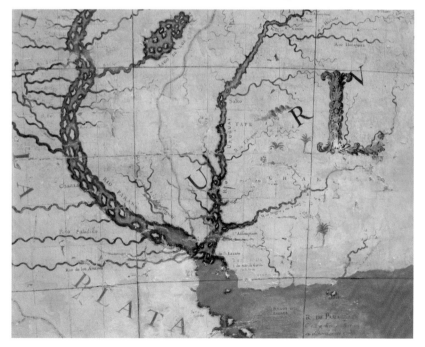

When Magellan encountered the entrance of Rio del Plata, South America, he hoped it would be his passage through the Pacific Ocean.

Ferdinand Magellan

Magellan discovered for his new nation and its king, Charles.

The ships proceeded slowly down the eastern coast of South America, and the pilots made careful notations in their logbooks of exactly where they were according to the star charts. Magellan still did not trust his officers well enough to tell them his plans, and three of the captains became increasingly angry with him because he was so secretive. They feared he planned to meet Portuguese agents somewhere, betray Spain, and give over command of the voyage to them.

When they came to the Rio del Plata, located between today's Argentina and Uruguay, Magellan hoped it was the passage through South America because it was so wide. He sent the *Santiago* to investigate. Two weeks later, the ship came back with the disappointing news that the Rio del Plata was simply a river.

It was now mid-March, the beginning of winter in the Southern **Hemisphere**. They were below 45 degrees **latitude** and sailing toward the South Pole. (The equivalent spot in the Northern Hemisphere would be Chicago.) The men were not prepared for winter. Most of them came from the Mediterranean area, where it was always warm. Storms followed, and the ships were showing damage. Magellan knew they had to find a place to stay for the winter, one protected from the storms and close to a source of food.

Magellan found a place and named this area of the Argentine coast Patagonia, which is Spanish for "big feet." Theory speculates that Magellan chose the name Patagonia because the Tehuelche people, who were native to the area, had large feet. They stood between six and seven feet (1.8–2.1 meters) tall. They would have appeared as giants to the men of southern Europe, who were much shorter than most men are today, probably under five feet five inches (1.6 m) tall.

Sparking a Mutiny

Meanwhile, Magellan's relationship with Captain Cartagena had gotten worse. One day, Cartagena was especially rude to Magellan in front of the other officers. Magellan ordered him arrested and took away his command of the *San Antonio*. Magellan wanted to watch Cartagena and thus imprisoned him on the deck of the *Trinidad*. The captain of the *Victoria* begged Magellan to place Cartagena in his custody, and Magellan consented, saying that the captain must promise that Cartagena would be kept on the ship. The captain agreed but then let Cartagena go ashore once they reached Brazil. Magellan arrested him again and transferred him to the *Concepcion*.

As they sailed south, Cartagena complained about the cold, lack of food, storms, and uncertainty of where they were headed. He pressed the other officers to insist to Magellan that they return to Spain. Magellan said he would not even consider returning home. He felt that would be a slap in the face to King Charles and the Casa, who had invested so much in this voyage. He could not disappoint them. He told the officers he would rather die because he prized honor above all else, including comfort.

On March 31, the convoy turned into a bay at 49 degrees south. Magellan knew they couldn't stand the cold if they went farther south, so he decided they would stay in this harbor, which he named Port San Julián. Furious at the decision, Cartagena attempted a **mutiny**, telling the men that Magellan was leading them to destruction. He promised them that they would get food and could return to Spain if they followed him. Even though they wanted to go home, most of the men were loyal to Magellan, who was able to end the mutiny after only a few hours.

Magellan immediately called a court martial for Cartagena and the men who supported him. Magellan did not preside over the trial; instead, a Spanish captain did. This was a wise move on Magellan's part. Cartagena and the mutineers were found guilty by a fellow countryman. One captain was sentenced to death. Cartagena was imprisoned. Almost forty other seamen were chained and sentenced to hard labor.

There was much labor to be done at Port San Julián. The crew had to clean and repair the ships and consolidate the supplies. Rotten boards were replaced, seams were caulked, and the hulls were tarred. An inventory of the supplies showed that the sailors had been cheated in Seville and had only half of what they needed. Their food supply would last only another six months.

It is difficult to understand why the men were unable to get food on shore. There were ostriches, llamas, rabbits, and other animals around, but the men had no success in hunting. Perhaps they were afraid to risk tasting the fruit, nuts, or roots they found, or perhaps they didn't find any. There was little freshwater to replenish their barrels. The water they found was salty and undrinkable.

When Magellan realized they had enough food for only a few more months, he knew they couldn't spend the whole winter in Port San Julián. They had to find a way to get to the western ocean and the Spice Islands, even though the weather was against them. It was so cold that many men suffered from frostbitten hands, and several men froze to death.

Cartagena tried one more time to get the men to mutiny. This time they were disgusted with him and didn't listen. Magellan sentenced him to be **marooned**. He and one other sailor were deposited on the coast of Patagonia with their swords and some food. Cartagena was never heard from again.

Before they left Port San Julián, Magellan sent the *Santiago* to explore a river inlet to the south. The ship ran into a violent squall that ripped off its sails. The crew was able to jump off onto the nearby beach. Minutes later, the ship was pounded to pieces in the surf. There were only four ships remaining. For eight days, the shipwrecked sailors collected timber from the ship. They'd planned to make a raft large enough to carry all of them back to Port San Julián. Weak with cold and hunger, they couldn't do it. Instead, they built a two-man raft, and the two strongest men were chosen for the journey. It took them eleven days to reach Magellan, and when they reached camp, they were so thin no one recognized them. Magellan sent a rescue party to bring back the other crewmen.

On August 24, the fleet left Port San Julián and continued south to an inlet they named Santa Cruz. There they found fish and seals to hunt. They enjoyed watching the penguins, which they called ducks. For the moment they had enough food. They spent the winter in the bay, and then left on October 18.

Finding a Channel

On October 21, the lookout spotted an opening that looked like a bay. The ships sailed in to investigate. The *San Antonio* and the *Concepción* went ahead to explore, while the *Trinidad* and *Victoria* waited. When they were satisfied that this was the passage to the sea, the first two ships returned with pennants flying, crews cheering, and guns firing.

Magellan named the passage All Saints Channel, but it would be forever known as the Strait of Magellan. Although Magellan and his crew had great hopes that it would be an easy passage to Balboa's Sea, it was not. It took them thirty-eight days to maneuver through the 334-mile (537 km) strait, bucking high winds and bitter cold. Rock cliffs and snow-capped mountains surrounded them. It looked like a place where no one could survive. Yet on the land to the south of them, they could see campfires burning

After months of searching, Magellan had finally found his passage to the Pacific Ocean, a passage which would later become known as Magellan's Strait.

at night. They named this area Tierra del Fuego, meaning "land of fire." This is the southernmost tip of South America.

Once they had found the strait, the men wanted to return home. They did not care about finding the Spice Islands or anything else. Again, Magellan stood firm. He insisted that they must go forward and do what they had promised.

One captain did not agree. Abruptly, and without telling the others, the *San Antonio* turned around in the strait and returned to Spain. This was a death warrant for many of the sailors on the other ships because the *San Antonio* was the supply ship that stored most of the food. When they arrived in Spain, the officers on the *San Antonio* were put in prison for deserting their duty.

Although it took the crewmen a little more than a month, the three ships eventually reached the western entrance of the channel, and beyond it, the vast ocean. Magellan's remaining fleet sailed into this new body of water on November 28. He was so pleased to find the calm ocean that he named it *Mar Pacifica*, meaning "soothing, peaceful ocean." The name has remained to this day, yet another legacy of Magellan's journey.

Chapter 6

Traversing the Pacific

While reaching the Pacific Ocean was an amazing achievement for Magellan and the crew of his three remaining ships, their journey was about to enter a new and challenging phase.

Although Magellan had finally found a way into the Pacific Ocean, there was still thousands of miles of open ocean between his fleet and its destination.

Sailing the vast ocean would prove fatal for many of the remaining sailors. Optimistically, Magellan thought his ships would reach the Spice Islands in less than a week. However, it would take about a year. During that period, the crew would endure dealing with a lack of food and water, coping with diseases, and fighting a number of battles.

The three ships sailed for three months and twenty days without fresh food. The water stored in the wooden barrels on deck rotted, and the crews couldn't drink salt water because it would kill them. Every day was a struggle to endure. After a couple of months, dead bodies were thrown overboard with regularity.

Pigafetta wrote: "We ate biscuit, which was no longer biscuit, but powder of biscuits swarming with worms, for they had eaten of good (it stank strongly of the urine of rats). We also ate some ox hides that covered the top of the main yard to prevent the yard from chafing the shrouds ... and often we ate sawdust from boards. Rats were sold for one-half ducat apiece, if only we could get them."

The most serious illness facing the sailors was **scurvy**, caused by vitamin C deficiency. Finding vitamin C was not an option for the sailors. Toward the end of the fifteenth century, scurvy became the major cause of disability and mortality among sailors on long sea voyages. The first symptoms to affect the men were swollen, sore, and bleeding gums. Their teeth loosened and fell out. Soon the men's joints and bones began to ache, and they suffered from an overall weakness.

Pigafetta wrote, "The gums of both lower and upper teeth of some of our men swelled, so that they could not eat under any circumstances and therefore died ... Twenty-five or thirty men [ached] in the arms, legs, or in another place, so that few remained well."

What saved Magellan and his officers from scurvy, although they didn't know it, was their supply of quince jelly. Just a tablespoon now and then contained enough vitamin C to keep them healthy. Magellan probably would have shared the jelly with his men if he had known how important it was.

The ships also suffered, and the sick men had to work to keep them afloat, operating the bilge pumps for hours at a time. Shipworms attacked the wood, causing leaks that had to be caulked. Fortunately, there were few storms. The Pacific was indeed pacific for their crossing.

Fish are bountiful in the Pacific, tuna and flying fish especially, yet the sailors didn't have nets to catch them. There are hundreds of islands in the Pacific filled with game, freshwater, fruits, and vegetables. Magellan and his men came within a few miles of some of these islands, yet the only ones they saw were barren and deserted.

A survivor reported that, toward the end of January, Magellan became so disgusted with Faleiro's star charts that he threw them overboard. On December 19, the sailors lost sight of the coast of South America. It wasn't until March 6, 1521, that they heard the welcome words, "Land ho!" The land they found was the tiny island of Guam, one of many islands in what would later be called the Mariana Islands. Today, Guam is a territory of the United States.

It is little wonder it was so difficult to find land during their journey though the Pacific Ocean. The Pacific Ocean takes up one-third of Earth's surface and is the largest of the world's oceans. In fact, it is twice the size of the Atlantic. The mean depth is 14,040 feet (4,280 m), or almost 3 miles (5 km). There are 30,000 islands of varying sizes scattered throughout the ocean. From the coast of South America to Malaysia, where Magellan was headed, is 12,000 miles (19,312 km). This is four times the mileage from New York to San Francisco. In 1521, this area was entirely uncharted.

The Native people of Guam, the Chamorro, came out in outrigger canoes to greet the ships. They appeared, as Pigafetta described them, "like dolphins leaping from wave to wave." They clambered aboard and quickly helped themselves to everything they could carry, despite the protests of the crew. The Chamorro even took one of the longboats, moving much faster than the weakened Europeans.

Outraged, Magellan ordered his men to fire blanks from the cannons to scare the Chamorro. As a result, relations between the two peoples were damaged. When the Spaniards later landed on the island, they were met with stones and spears, not friendship. The armored soldiers set fire to a village of fifty houses and killed seven people. Then they helped themselves to coconuts, fruit, and freshwater.

Magellan named the place "Island of Thieves." Today, we know that the Chamorro were not thieves but believed in sharing in a way that Europeans could not understand. The Chamorro assumed that they could help themselves to whatever they found because they allowed others to take whatever they wanted. They did not understand the idea of private property.

Reinvigorated at last by freshwater, fruit, and fish, the convoy set sail again. They came to a larger island, Samar, the westernmost of the Philippine Islands. Crewmembers were unable to land because coral reefs ringed the coast. The sharp coral would have torn the hulls of the ships.

The next island going east, Suluan, had a sandy beach. Magellan ordered tents put up for the men with scurvy. He stayed aboard the *Trinidad* but went ashore every day to see how the men were doing. He even gave them coconut milk to sip.

The Complications with Navigation

The first rule of navigation is to know where you are. The second is to know where you want to go. Only then can you figure out how to get there. On the open sea, it is impossible to tell where you are if you don't have instruments that measure distance.

Navigation today is a mathematical science dependent on computerized instruments and sonar, an underwater radar system. But for hundreds of years, it was based on experience and eyesight alone.

An important part of ancient navigation was determining the speed of a vessel. Knowing how fast the ship is traveling helps the captain and navigator know how much distance the ship has covered in a given time, which in turn helps determine the location of the ship on the open ocean. Sailors in Magellan's time figured their ship's speed by tossing a log over the prow (front) of the ship and timing with an hourglass how long it took to reach the stern (back). This very simple system did not produce accurate results, but it gave sailors a general idea of how fast their ship was moving.

Another practice the ancients used to navigate was dead reckoning, or guessing where you are based on landmarks. On the open ocean, however, there are no landmarks, but there are signposts in the sky.

After a few days, a craft carrying people native to the area approached the camp. Magellan welcomed them and gave them cloth, combs, mirrors, bells, and other trinkets. The men were tattooed and wore cotton skirts embroidered with silk. They brought fish, chickens, bananas, and oranges to the hungry men.

Many of the sick men regained their strength, and the convoy set off again on March 22, 1521. Less than a week later, the ship was approached by eight people, native to the area, in a canoe. They were more timid than the other Native people the

In 140 CE, an Egyptian named Ptolemy devised a mathematical system for using the stars to determine location. This system is called celestial navigation. Using celestial navigation, sailors could estimate their position by pinpointing the known stars in a clear night sky or, by day, measuring the height of the Sun. This told them how close they were to the equator, which is the imaginary line that runs around the middle of Earth at zero degrees latitude. Using this information, they could estimate their ship's latitude if they had a fairly reliable instrument to measure the height of the Sun or a given star.

There were problems with this method, however. When the stars or sun are obscured, such as on a cloudy night or stormy day, for example, this method does not work. Also, although the night sky of the Northern Hemisphere was well known to Europeans by Magellan's time, the constellations of the Southern Hemisphere were not. Once his ships got out of familiar territory, they had no celestial signposts to guide them.

The ancient Greeks thought up the idea of latitude and longitude—dividing Earth into squares—but it was just a guessing game until proven by navigators. In Magellan's day, longitude could not be determined, in part because no one knew Earth's size. Magellan's contributions to navigation helped make the measurement of longitude possible.

crewmen had encountered. Magellan and his slave Enrique, who could speak their language, convinced them to come aboard. Incidentally, Enrique, a native of the Philippines, had at this point become the first man to circumnavigate the globe.

Their chief was Colambu. He brought them gold and ginger, both items of great interest to the Europeans. Magellan told Colambu he wanted friendly and peaceful relations. Colambu then insisted that they become blood brothers, which they did. Over the next few days, Magellan and Colambu forged

Many of the Natives Magellan encountered were friendly and receptive to the idea of converting to Christianity. However, Magellan's presence would later lead to violence.

a great friendship. This friendship, however, would bring about Magellan's death.

Converting Locals to Christianity

March 31, 1521, was Easter Sunday on the Christian calendar. The Europeans came ashore dressed in their finest clothes. While the attentive natives of the island watched, the Europeans conducted a solemn mass. The religious ceremony impressed Colambu, who wanted to participate. Afterward, Magellan gave Colambu a tall cross to be put on the highest point of the island. It would serve as a signal to men on other Spanish ships that they would be received as friends. In that way, Magellan claimed the Philippine Islands for Spain, calling them Mazaua.

The gold jewelry that Colambu and his family wore made Magellan think of the fabled King Solomon's mines, according to a survivor's report of the expedition. Later, a Spaniard claimed that on one island there were gold nuggets the size of hazelnuts and they could be sifted from the sand. Gold was not something

Ferdinand Magellan

Magellan had considered he would find; he had thought only of spices. Perhaps the gold made him more eager to secure the islands for Spain.

Colambu told Magellan that the island of Cebu was a center for the Asian spice trade, with ships stopping from all over Asia. Magellan decided that this should be their next stop. On April 7, 1521, with banners and pennants flying, his three ships pulled into the busy port and fired a salute. Colambu's friend, Rajah Humabon, was the ruler of the island. Humabon greeted them warmly. They sat on chairs covered with red velvet and negotiated a treaty. Magellan talked to the chief and his ministers about Christianity. They seemed interested.

On April 14, 1521, a special ceremony of baptism was held in Cebu City. A large platform, draped with bright tapestries and decorated with palm leaves, was built for Magellan. He dressed in a white robe as a symbol of his love for those who were about to convert and become Christians. Magellan then gave a long sermon about Christianity. Afterward, about 800 of the people native to Mazaua, including Humabon and Colambu and their families, were baptized.

After the long, grueling trip with officers who mistrusted him, Magellan felt great satisfaction from the faith the Native people put in him and his religion, but it made him want more. He wanted to make everyone on all the islands Christian.

Chieftains from other islands in the Philippines were not as impressed with Magellan as Humabon and Colambu were. They refused to bring a tribute or be baptized. Rajah (king) Lapulapu was especially defiant and said he had no interest in becoming a Christian. This time Magellan's officers gave him good advice: "Forget about it, leave him alone." Humabon agreed with the officers, but Magellan refused to listen.

When Magellan tried to force Christianity on all of the Natives of the Phillippines, many fought back, eventually killing Magellan.

Magellan was sure he could force Lapulapu and his people to accept Christianity. To prove his point, he took a party of forty-eight men ashore in order to launch an attack. However, Magellan and his party found the Native people prepared to fight back, using weapons of stones, arrows, and spears.

For several hours on the morning of April 27, 1521, neither side could gain an advantage. Magellan's men soon ran out of ammunition. Magellan then ordered his men to retreat, but he would not make it back to the ship with his crew. Lapulapu's people shot Magellan with a poisoned arrow and eventually Magellan was killed with a spear through his throat. Magellan would not live to see his expedition complete its journey around the world.

Ferdinand Magellan

Chapter 7

Completing the Journey

I n early September 1522, the *Victoria*, with a crew of just twenty-one, reached the mouth of Spain's Guadalquivir River. Almost three years since Magellan's fleet had embarked on its quest, the sole ship returned with only seventeen of its original sailors, along with a

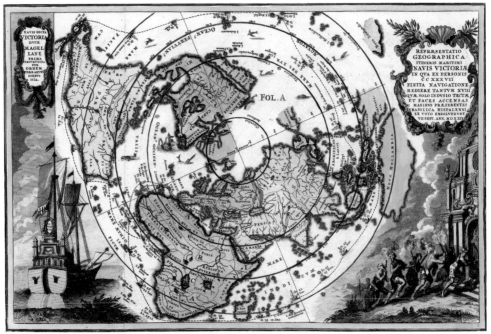

Magellan's voyage around the globe came at a great cost, incuding Magellan's own life, but his explorations went a long way toward expanding knowledge of the shape, size, and nature of the world.

few Malaysians that had joined during the journey. The original master of the *Concepcion*, Juan Sebastian de Elcano, was now serving as captain of the *Victoria*. Unlike today, where Magellan receives credit for the journey, de Elcano was the one lauded in Spain for completing the circumnavigation.

The *Victoria's* topmast had been damaged in a storm. Her timbers were worm-eaten and heavy with barnacles, and her seams were leaking badly. The small crew had to continuously pump water from the ship just to stay afloat. A boat came out to guide them into the harbor of Sanlúcar de Barrameda. *Victoria* arrived in Seville on Monday, September 8, 1522. The crew fired their artillery in a final salute and then debarked.

As they had promised during their ordeal, those of the crew who could walk made a pilgrimage to the shrine of Nuestra Señora de la Victoria and then to the church of Santa Maria la Antigua. Barefoot, in rags, carrying candles, and weeping, they made a sad procession.

After Magellan's death, the crew's voyage back to Spain from the Philippines had been long and terrible. The rotting *Concepcion* had so few crew members that the captain ordered it burned. Portuguese forces captured the *Trinidad* and imprisoned her crew. Violent storms and malnutrition also took their toll on the crew. Nonetheless, what was left of the expedition reached the Spice Islands as promised and brought back a cargo of cloves.

The survivors were welcomed in the court of King Charles V, now the emperor of Western Europe. He was pleased with the treaty signed by the Moluccan rulers. It promised prosperity for Spain. Ironically, he had just married the sister of João III of Portugal and had ended the Spanish competition with that country.

Charles continued to support voyages of exploration for Spain, but most of his attention was focused on keeping the

Catholic countries of Europe together. The Protestant Reformation was spreading and seemed a serious threat to the Holy Roman Empire. Some of the surviving sailors from Magellan's voyage petitioned the court years later because they still had not received their pay. No one got rich from the expedition, and several never recovered their health.

The political gain from Magellan's voyage was fairly small, although it would be long-lived. Later expeditions secured the Philippine Islands for Spain, and Spain would hold them until 1898, when the Spanish-American War freed the islands from Spanish rule and made them a protectorate of the United States.

The Spice Islands were the site of skirmishes between many nations for the next century, with the Dutch finally winning. By the end of the eighteenth century, the demand for spices had decreased and the islands were no longer important to Europeans.

Spanish explorers, conquistadors (conquerors), and colonists made the South American continent solidly Spanish from Mexico to Tierra del Fuego. Brazil remained Portuguese. In the nineteenth century, all of the Latin American countries founded by Europeans became independent nations.

Magellan, as Viewed by His Contemporaries

By every measure in 1522, Magellan's voyage was a failure. He was blamed for the deaths of many men and for mistakes in navigation. Neither Spain nor Portugal wanted to claim him. Both countries scorned him. The strait that he spent so long searching for did not make a difference to the business of trade. It was all but ignored for years.

His wife and son were both dead by the time the *Victoria* returned. Beatriz's father, Diego Barbosa, made a claim for a share of the proceeds from the sale of the cargo in her name, but it was rejected. None of the family, including Magellan's brother and sister, received a penny from the venture. The merchants who invested in the voyage, however, did receive their money back. They also earned a small profit after the cloves were sold.

Most of the survivors of the voyage, called Magellan a tyrant and a poor commander. So did those from the *San Antonio*, which had turned back for Spain at the Strait of Magellan. Only a few people supported him. One was Antonio Pigafetta. Pigafetta traveled across Europe trying to get people to read his journal so they would understand that Magellan was an able commander and a good sailor. The diary was not published until after Pigafetta's death. Hundreds of years later, a few people read it. When they did, general feelings about Magellan started to change.

A crewmember who also thought Magellan was a good commander was "the Genoese pilot," the pilot of the *Trinidad*. His logbook was saved and shows that Pigafetta told the truth about the important events, such as the mutiny in Port San Julián and the concern that Magellan had for his men.

The ships themselves met tragic fates. While the *Trinidad*'s crew was being held by the Portuguese in the Spice Islands, the ship was hit by a storm and broke into pieces. The *Victoria*, the only surviving ship of the expedition, made two later voyages to Santo Domingo in the New World. Returning to Seville from the last of these voyages, she and all men on board were lost.

Magellan's Discoveries

Although he was a target of disrespect for years, Magellan is now ranked with Columbus as one of the prime explorers in the Age of Discovery. His findings changed how people everywhere thought about their world. Thanks to Magellan, people in the

South Seas were introduced to Europe, and people in Europe were introduced to the islands of the Pacific.

Magellan's most important achievement is that he gave us a realistic perception of the size of Earth, its enormous seas, and the way its landmasses are distributed. This is something we take for granted today, but in 1522, it was a wonderful surprise. People had to erase their old ideas about Earth and look at it in a new way.

Magellan showed that the world's oceans are connected. This meant that world trade was possible on a scale never before imagined. This fact also proved to be very important to the world's military leaders. It spurred the building of oceangoing ships in the small countries of northern Europe and generated ideas of world conquest and great wealth. A popular saying was that "whoever controlled the oceans controlled the world."

Magellan and his men gave names to hundreds of rivers, capes, islands, and mountains. In this way, they left their imprint all along their route. Reminders of the voyage can be found all along the eastern coast of South America.

Magellan Leaves a Scientific Legacy

The scientific results of Magellan's voyage were far more important than were the political or economic ones, and scientists continue to honor him today. Magellan insisted that careful records be kept of every move of the journey, with times and places recorded. Many of these logbooks and charts were lost, but enough were saved to enable scientists to reconstruct the voyage in detail.

Largely as a result of Magellan's voyage, navigators and geographers perfected a system of latitude and longitude, although it would take 250 years to happen. Magellan proved that these imaginary lines are valid and that they enable travelers

Magellan's Shrine, shown here, was erected in 1866 in Cebu, Phillippines, around the spot where Magellan was killed.

to know where they are and how to get where they are going, even when there are no landmarks. This led to the development of world travel in ways no one could have envisioned in 1522. Latitude and longitude also allow geographers, **seismologists**, and oceanographers to pinpoint oceanic disturbances and ecological problems.

Astronomers honored the explorer by naming the small galaxies that line the Milky Way, the Magellanic Clouds. These "clouds" are visible only in the Southern Hemisphere, and Magellan was the first European navigator to make note of them.

In 1989, the National Aeronautics and Space Administration (NASA) named the first spacecraft to map the surface of Venus, *Magellan*. The space probe provided the first detailed global map of that planet. It burned up in the atmosphere of Venus in 1994.

The strait that Magellan labored to find in present-day Chile still bears his name, and near it stands Universidad de Magallanes.

Magellan is also honored with a monument in the Philippines, although the Native chief Lapulapu is also honored with a monument as well. Just as Magellan is now an iconic hero to his people, people native to the Philippines also revere their former chief Lapulapu, who stood up to an invading outsider.

Magellan may not have gained great wealth or fame from his journey, which actually claimed his life, but it left a lasting legacy to this day.

Timeline

1480
Ferdinand Magellan is born in Portugal.

1488
Bartolomeu Dias rounds the Cape of Good Hope at the southern tip of Africa.

1492
Funded by Spain, Christopher Columbus reaches the New World.

1494
Magellan serves in Lisbon as a page in the court of King João II.

1499
Vasco da Gama returns from India.

1500
Pedro Álvares Cabral explores Brazil.

1505
Magellan sails for the Indies with Dom Francisco de Almeida.

1506
Magellan is wounded in battle.

1509
Magellan is again wounded in battle.

1510
Magellan is promoted to captain in the Portuguese army.

1511

The Portuguese army captures Malacca, giving Portuguese traders access to spices.

1512

Magellan studies routes to the Spice Islands.

1513

Vasco Nuñez de Balboa sights the Pacific Ocean from a mountain in Panama.

1517

After being accused of trading with the enemy, Magellan leaves Portugal for Spain.

1518

Magellan presents his idea of finding a route to the Pacific Ocean to King Charles I of Spain.

1518

Magellan prepares five ships for a voyage to the Spice Islands.

1519

Magellan's voyage begins.

1521

Magellan is killed in the Philippine Islands.

1522

The *Victoria*, the last remaining ship in Magellan's expedition, returns to Spain after sailing around the world.

Glossary

armament A military unit and its supplies.

astrolabe An early scientific instrument used to determine the altitude of the Sun.

carrack A stout merchant ship used in the fifteenth century; also called a não.

cartographer A person who makes maps.

chart A map of maritime and coastal areas used by sailors to navigate.

celestial navigation Finding one's way using the positions of the stars as a guide.

circumnavigate To sail completely around the world.

equator An imaginary line at zero degrees latitude that circles Earth at its widest point.

hemisphere One-half of the Earth. The Northern Hemisphere lies north of the equator, and the Southern Hemisphere lies south of the equator.

latitude The imaginary lines that circle the globe to the east and west, parallel to the equator.

line of demarcation A political border often used to define the limits of disputing nations. In 1494, the Treaty of Tordesillas created a line of demarcation dividing the New World between Spain and Portugal.

longitude The imaginary lines that circle the globe to the north and south, from pole to pole.

maroon To abandon.

mutiny To revolt against a ship's captain.

nobility People born into high class or rank.

ordinary seaman The lowest rank of sailor on a ship.

page A youthful attendant to a person of rank.

scurvy One of the oldest-known nutritional disorders of humankind—also called vitamin C deficiency. It destroys the body's soft tissue, beginning with the gums, and was the scourge of sailors until the mid-eighteenth century.

seismologist A scientist who studies earthquakes and Earth.

strait A narrow passage especially between two large bodies of water.

For More Information

Books

Bergreen, Laurence. *Over the Edge of the World*. New York, NY: Harper Collins, 2008.

Lyons, Amy. *Ferdinand Magellan 168 Success Facts—Everything You Need to Know about Ferdinand Magellan*. Brisbane, Australia: Emereo Publishing, 2014.

Waldman, Stuart. *Magellan's World*. Great Explorers. New York, NY: Mikaya Press, 2007.

Websites

The History Channel's Ferdinand Magellan page
www.history.com/topics/exploration/ferdinand-magellan
Take a quick look at Magellan and his voyage to reach Asia by sailing through the Atlantic and Pacific Oceans. Watch several short videos about Magellan and other explorers.

The Mariner's Museum: Ferdinand Magellan
ageofex.marinersmuseum.org
Retrace the steps of great explorers, learn about their tools of navigation, read about their ships, and more. Learn more about Ferdinand Magellan, accounts of his voyages, and illustrations of the places he visited. Explore the interactive map of his voyages.

Polynesian History and Origin
www.pbs.org/wayfinders/polynesian.html
When European explorers first ventured into the Pacific, they were surprised to find thriving societies of people still living in the Stone Age. Find out where these people came from, how they reached the islands, and more by exploring this companion website to the film *Wayfinders: A Pacific Odyssey*.

Index